Living With Her

Everything you need to know

Alex Hallatt

summersdale

Living With Her

Summersdale Publishers Ltd
46 West Street
Chichester
West Sussex
PO19 1RP
UK

www.summersdale.com

Printed and bound in Belgium

ISBN 1 84024 449 6

Thank you to the guys who helped me write this book:

Matt, CJ and especially Andy, Cliff, Tim and Dale, whose contributions were inspired.

Contents

INTRODUCTION

Your mates think you're seeing things through magnolia-tinted glasses, but you know you're on to a good thing with this woman. Living together feels like the natural next step for the relationship. It is also a hell of a lot cheaper than living apart. With skill and foresight, couples can live together for years without any long-term ill effects like marriage or children.

Perhaps you are currently living apart and considering whether living together is the right thing to do, or maybe you have already moved in with your girl and want to know how to maintain the initial domestic bliss. Either way, this book will prove invaluable in helping you to understand her and avoid potential cohabitation pitfalls.

Keep it in the bathroom as a handy reference manual... only keep it away from the hair-removal wax.

PRACTICALITIES

NUTRITION

The beer to spring water ratio
of the fridge contents will
change disturbingly.

Men need more calories than women, so it is fair for you to have bigger helpings of the pizza, chips and Chinese takeaways.

When she is on a diet, so are you. Forget visits to McDonald's, the late-night garage or the chippy, unless you can incorporate them into a dog walk/'emergency visit to a desperate friend'/fake sleepwalk.

Drinking direct from milk/
juice cartons is NOT allowed.
Unless you can do it without
getting caught.

You used to get your whole week's grocery shopping done in one basket. Now it takes a large, wobbly-wheeled trolley, four supermarket visits, or both.

Cans of unidentifiable, bargain-buy foods and obscure ingredients will accumulate on the back shelf of the cupboard. Don't ask what she needs these for: it may precipitate a nutritional health kick.

HOUSEWORK

Whereas both of you may have lived in clean, tidy places before, it is no guarantee that your home together will be the same. If you can't afford a cleaner, you need to know the following:

Cleaning

If she sees your favourite old handkerchief lying on the bedroom floor, she will maliciously vacuum it up rather than put it in the laundry basket.

Tidying

No, she is not hiding your address book, TV remote or lads' mags: she is 'tidying'.

Cooking

Her cooking is likely to follow the tastes of the celebrity chef du jour and will take so long to prepare that you will have to stave off severe hunger pangs with nuts, crisps, pretzels, chocolates and any other loose items in the cupboard.

Washing-up

The male tolerance limit for hot water temperatures is on average 10–15 degrees below that for females. Never *ever* plunge your hands into the sink she filled, unless you have at least two sets of rubber gloves on or some frozen peas close by.

It's fair that the person not cooking washes up. It's not fair for the cook to use every last pot, pan and utensil in the kitchen.

Living together can mean more wholesome, healthy meals – until you develop a habit of eating out or getting takeaway nearly every night to save arguments over the washing up.

Laundry

It's every man's mission in life to wear his boxers/underpants for as many consecutive days as possible. Tell her this cuts down on washing and therefore is better for the environment.

There will always be a rogue pair of red knickers that find their way into the whites: unless you like pink pants, take your smalls round to your mum's.

DIY

By eliminating the inter-lover commute, you should have more time to enjoy yourselves, right? Wrong: all this time and more will be spent on home improvements, and any time not spent on home improvements will be spent watching home improvement TV.

DIY causes no end of arguments, even if it is only about what colour the living room should be painted. This is why so many couples are surrounded by 'shades of white' walls. Then there are the health hazards: paint fumes; sharp, rotating blades; nail guns pointed at your head in response to your offer of some basic tuition...

You'll spend hours going through Ikea looking for the one item you liked in the catalogue. Then, back home, you'll realise you're missing one vital, weird-shaped woggly thingumijig, which cannot be posted to you and which will force you to negotiate the store again.

Before embarking on any home improvements, consider that...

... you have to live with the person you are DIY-ing with; don't upset her by criticising the bad choice of colour scheme. Reassure her that it isn't her fault – how was she to know that 'biscuit beige' would look like a dog had thrown up on the walls?

... the Swedish meatballs in Ikea's restaurant are very addictive. Several visits there and you'll need a bigger wardrobe.

... working on home improvements with your loved one will let her see more of your talents – especially how inventive you can be with expletives.

It is worth employing professionals for: a) electrical work; b) plumbing; and c) anything else – life is too short.

MONEY

It's a myth that bills for two are cheaper than for one. This will be a bone of contention however you decide to share the household expenses. If you take turns to pay bills or buy the groceries, the more conscientious one will inevitably end up out of pocket.

On the other hand, if you get a joint account, all will be well. For the first month. After this, the account that was only to be used for the mortgage, utilities and groceries will now also be used for cosmetic dentistry, pedicures and subscriptions to *Marie Claire*.

SEX AND ROMANCE

Remember the golden rule: when a couple is living together, the woman can have sex whenever she wants it; the man can have sex whenever the woman wants it.

Toenail clipping may improve your appearance, but it has not been recognised as a sexy activity, especially not in bed. And farting in bed is a proven anti-aphrodisiac. These habits are to be avoided if you want to significantly improve your chances of getting lucky.

To remain sexually attractive, it is important to continue to take pride in your appearance. Don't expect her to jump your bones when your sexiest evening wear consists of only your big, grey, comfy underpants.

You seemed to have sex all the time before you moved in together, but now when you feel like it she will be rushing off to work and you will be left... er... hanging. To avoid frustration, make time for sex and write it in her diary or on her wall planner in the office.

Even though you sleep together in the same bed, she will still complain that the relationship is dying. You might have thought that living with her was an act of love itself, but unfortunately it won't get you out of Valentine's Day, anniversaries or spontaneous romantic gestures.

CONVERSATION

Never ever say 'Yes, dear...'

Fear-inducing questions about your 'future' are likely to be lobbed at you with no warning. The best approach to this is to say you will talk about it later. With any luck, you won't have to specify exactly when 'later' is.

However, be warned that these issues may suddenly assume paramount importance at 3 a.m. You may be required to answer deep and philosophical questions relating to 'where we are going'. Failure to do so at this early hour is unwise, despite your semi-conscious condition.

Living with you doesn't make her any more interested in talking about cars, bikes or sport. She just doesn't bother to hide it now.

If you do run out of things to say to each other, all is not lost – you might just need a bigger TV.

GUIDELINES

TERRITORY

The entire house or flat is effectively under her reign. You may think you have dibs on the loo because you spend more time in there, but in fact you only control the garage, shed or other outdoor buildings, if you have them. In some instances, you may also be able to count the basement and/or attic as part of your realm, but only if gaining access involves at least one ladder and/or one human-sized spider web near the entrance.

Weird ornaments and trinkets, which are neither useful nor attractive, will colonise previously empty horizontal surfaces in the house because they're 'lovely' or of 'sentimental value'.

Get two duvets and save a lot of tussles and cold feet. You might still want to staple yours to your side of the bed, as she will try and steal it anyway.

Don't expect an equal share of the wardrobe. A lot of the space will be taken up by a ridiculous number of shoes, many of which cause her physical pain and an even bigger proportion of which will be worn only once.

The garden patio isn't just for barbecues and drinking beer. You may need to allow her some space for useless things like flowers.

Meanwhile, she will also start using a perfectly serviceable chair as a makeshift wardrobe, allowing clothing to accumulate on it to the point where she can't find anything to wear and you can't find anywhere to sit.

You may convince her that you really do need a Dolby Digital 5.1 surround sound system with active subwoofer and rear ceiling-mounted speakers. However, you will soon realise that such strict limits apply to the volume control that you might as well have kept that nice little television with the rabbit ears and built-in mono tweeter.

Don't question the number of jars, bottles and boxes in the bathroom cupboard unless you want a lecture on how you easy you have it, not having to maintain smooth legs or deal with 'having the painters in' every month.

LAWS OF PHYSICS

An object at rest tends to stay at rest.

Remind her that this should be respected when that object is sitting on the sofa, watching sport on TV.

An object in motion tends to stay in motion, unless acted upon by an unbalanced force.If she finds out that you used her face flannel to clean your pee from the loo seat you left down, she will become unbalanced and a force to be reckoned with: run and keep running.

E=mc²

Where *E* is excess weight gained, *m* is mass of couple at point of moving in together and *c* is cubic feet of fridge space.

Every action has an equal and opposite reaction.

Cheating on your partner will end in tears, even if it is only at *Scrabble*.

Not everything adds up.

The quantity of loo rolls used in a shared home is greater than the sum of loo rolls used before living together.

HOME RULES

1. Unlike a house share with your mates and constant visitors, it will be self-evident who left the empty loo roll tube on the holder, so you have to change it.

2. Sweaty gym kit cannot be dried in the bathroom for repeat wearing for the whole week.

3. Clothes can only be chucked on the floor in a moment of passion and will later have to find their way to the laundry bin.

4. Do not try to surreptitiously make a hot drink for one, at any time.

5. Don't expect her to have made dinner for you if you get home late. Especially if you are late because of a few after work drinks with your mates. *Especially* if you didn't call to say you would be late.

6. Bringing her flowers will get you lots of brownie points. Make sure that you do this even if you haven't done anything wrong, at least occasionally.

7. Her girly bed linen will get priority on the bed and yours will be stuffed into the inaccessible part of the airing cupboard.

8. No matter how many times you replay it, she won't be impressed with your PlayStation goal-scoring skills.

9. Your other half won't be pleased if you drink most of the juice and put the virtually empty container back in the fridge to avoid using the nearly full bin.

10. If the kitchen bin is full, you have to empty it. Your rubbish-balancing act may well be worthy of the Chinese State Circus but she is unlikely to see its artistic merit.

ADVANCED

DANGER ZONES

Children change everything. Domestic bliss can lull you into a false sense of security and you might not be as careful as you were before. If she misses a pill it is your fault for not reminding her. Neither can you rely on your supply of out-of-date condoms that you bought in your distant, optimistic past.

Even without children, no one sleeps better together than they do apart, even though they may like to think they do. What if you snore and she fidgets? Invest early in a supersize, separately sprung bed and earplugs. Or just cut out the 40 years of denial and get separate rooms.

THINGS NOT TO SAY

'So you're not a natural blonde, then?'

'Since you are ironing your clothes, can you do mine?' Moving in together does not get you a live-in maid, even if you get her to wear the uniform sometimes.

'I should get my mother to give you some recipes.'

THE END

You know you have been living together too long when:

🏠 you call sex 'that Tuesday night thing'.

🏠 you start to look alike... including matching moustaches.

🏠 she wears your underpants and it doesn't appear odd.

♠ you feel guilty watching more than five minutes of sport on TV, even if she is away for the weekend.

♠ she spends an hour talking to someone on the phone, only to hand it over to you, saying it's your mother.

♠ even the loo isn't private anymore...
... even for number twos.

AFTERWORD

Living with a woman is like servicing a well-loved car: by investing a little care and attention, you'll be able to enjoy the journey it takes you on, without suffering a breakdown. And if you do get a little lost en route, don't be afraid to consult this book for directions. Following them carefully, you'll be in for a great ride... and won't be driven crazy.

www.summersdale.com